Giant Octopus

GIANTS
of the
OCEAN

Alexis Roumanis

MEDIA ENHANCED BOOKS

AV2 BY WEIGL™

ADDED VALUE • AUDIO VISUAL

www.av2books.com

AV² provides enriched content that supplements and complements this book. Weigl's AV² books strive to create inspired learning and engage young minds in a total learning experience.

Your AV² Media Enhanced books come alive with...

Audio
Listen to sections of the book read aloud.

Key Words
Study vocabulary, and complete a matching word activity.

Video
Watch informative video clips.

Quizzes
Test your knowledge.

Go to www.av2books.com, and enter this book's unique code.

Embedded Weblinks
Gain additional information for research.

Slide Show
View images and captions, and prepare a presentation.

BOOK CODE

Q125605

AV² by Weigl brings you media enhanced books that support active learning.

Try This!
Complete activities and hands-on experiments.

... and much, much more!

Published by AV2 by Weigl
350 5th Avenue, 59th Floor New York, NY 10118
Websites: www.av2books.com   www.weigl.com

Library of Congress Cataloging-in-Publication Data

Roumanis, Alexis, author.
 Giant octopus / Alexis Roumanis.
     pages cm. -- (Giants of the ocean)
 Includes index.
 ISBN 978-1-4896-1070-6 (hardcover : alk. paper) -- ISBN 978-1-4896-1071-3 (softcover : alk. paper) --
ISBN 978-1-4896-1072-0 (single user ebk.) -- ISBN 978-1-4896-1073-7 (multi user ebk.)
 1. North Pacific giant octopus--Juvenile literature. 2. Octopuses--Juvenile literature. I. Title.
 QL430.3.O2R68 2014
 594.56--dc23
                                    2014004317

Printed in the United States of America in North Mankato, Minnesota
1 2 3 4 5 6 7 8 9 0 18 17 16 15 14

042014
WEP150314

Project Coordinator: Heather Kissock
Design: Mandy Christiansen

Weigl acknowledges Getty Images and Alamy as the primary image suppliers for this title.

Contents

Meet the Giant Octopus

The giant octopus is a type of mollusk that lives in the ocean. Mollusks are a group of **invertebrates** that includes more than 50,000 land-dwelling, freshwater, and marine **species**. Snails, scallops, and clams are all mollusks.

Giant octopuses have three hearts. This is more than any other species on the planet. Two hearts pump blood to the **gills**. The third heart pumps the blood throughout the giant octopus's body.

Giant octopuses can regrow their arms if they become damaged. A special **protein** helps new nerves to grow. This allows the octopus to gain full movement in its new arm. Growing the arm happens over time. The entire process takes about four months to complete.

Octopuses have a hose-like tube called a funnel that can spurt ink. The ink helps protect the octopus from **predators**. It forms a dark cloud around the octopus. Predators, such as sharks, cannot smell the octopus through the ink cloud.

Scientists now believe that two of the octopus's eight arms are legs. They use them to push off from surfaces.

All About the Giant Octopus

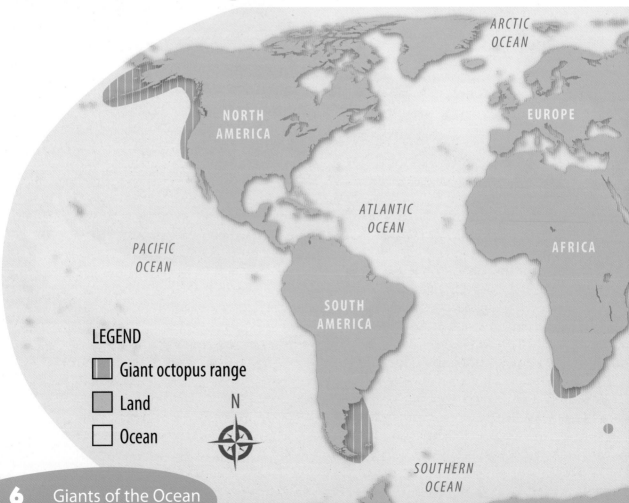

All octopuses are members of the Cephalopoda **class**. Cephalopods have a bird-like beak that is used to bite their prey. There are three types of giant octopus. These are the giant Pacific octopus, the southern giant octopus, and the southern red octopus. The giant Pacific octopus is the largest of the three. It can weigh up to 400 pounds (181 kilograms).

Where Giant Octopus Live

ARCTIC OCEAN

NORTH AMERICA

EUROPE

ATLANTIC OCEAN

PACIFIC OCEAN

AFRICA

SOUTH AMERICA

LEGEND

Giant octopus range

Land

Ocean

N

SOUTHERN OCEAN

ANTARCTICA

Octopus is actually a Greek word that means "eight-footed." The name describes the octopus's eight limbs. Each limb has many suckers. Giant Pacific octopuses have two rows of suckers that are used as sensors, for movement, and to capture prey.

Octopuses can fit into any opening bigger than their beak. This means that a 50-pound (23-kg) giant octopus can fit through a hole that is roughly 2 inches (5.1 centimeters) in diameter. The giant octopus uses this ability to catch prey.

9 to 16 feet (2.7 to 4.9 meters) long

Can weigh from about **22** to **400 pounds** (**10** to **181** kilograms).

The largest giant octopus ever caught measured **30 feet (9.1 m)** across and weighed more than **600 pounds** (272 kg).

Classifying the Giant Octopus

ORDER
Octopoda

FAMILY
Octopodidae

GENUS
Enteroctopus

SPECIES
Enteroctopus dofleini (giant Pacific octopus)

Enteroctopusmagnificus (southern giant octopus)

Enteroctopus megalocyathus (southern red octopus)

The Home of the Giant Octopus

All giant octopus species prefer regions with mild climates. The southern giant octopus is mostly found along the African coast, from Namibia to South Africa. Southern red octopuses live in the waters off the coast of South America, near Chile, Argentina, and the Falkland Islands. The giant Pacific octopus resides along the west coast of North America and the eastern coast of Asia. All three giant octopus species live in fairly shallow waters of about 330 feet (100 m), but they have been found at a depth of 3,281 feet (1,000 m).

Giant octopuses grow quickly. They **outgrow** their old homes and **must change dens** often.

Unlike many mollusks, octopuses do not have an outer shell to protect themselves from predators. This forces the octopus to find or create a den at the bottom of the ocean. Types of dens vary depending on what resources are available. Small octopuses have been known to use glass jars as dens. Larger octopuses often use a cluster of rocks. Sometimes, they dig under rocks and logs. Giant octopuses do not stay in one place for very long. Instead, they move from den to den.

Sometimes, a giant octopus will gather empty shells to seal off the entrance to its den. This is called an "octopus garden."

Features of the Giant Octopus

The giant octopus has **adapted** to its environment. It has several features that allow it to thrive in its watery **habitat**.

BEAK
An octopus's beak is made of the same material as human fingernails. Inside the beak is a tongue-like organ called a radula. The radula is covered in sharp teeth. The teeth are replaced whenever they wear out.

SKIN
An octopus can change the color of its skin. This process is controlled by muscles that send signals to individual **cells**. These cells contain **pigment** and are able to reflect light.

HEAD

Giant octopuses have large, bulbous heads. Their brains continue to increase in size throughout their entire lives. Many scientists believe the octopus is the most intelligent invertebrate.

MANTLE

The mantle is a muscled structure that contains the octopus's organs. It draws water over an octopus's gills, allowing the octopus to breathe. The water is drained out of the mantle and can then be used to propel the octopus away from predators.

SUCKERS

Giant octopuses have about 240 suckers on each of their eight legs. One 2.5-inch (6.4-cm) sucker is capable of lifting 35 pounds (15.9 kg) of weight.

Diet of the Giant Octopus

Giant octopuses are carnivores. Carnivores are animals that eat other animals. Giant octopuses feed mostly on crabs, scallops, snails, fish, and even sharks. They have several features that allow them to hunt these prey animals.

When food is scarce, giant octopuses will **eat members of their own species.**

Giant octopuses have two **salivary glands** in their mouths. One gland produces a **toxin**. When an octopus sees something it wants to eat, it squirts this toxin into the prey's gills. The toxin **paralyzes** the prey, making it easy to capture. Once the prey is caught, the second gland begins making substances that break down the prey.

If its prey is difficult to pull apart or bite into, a giant octopus can drill a hole into it. The octopus releases a substance onto the shell of its prey. This softens the shell until there is a small hole. The giant octopus's toxin then goes into the hole.

A giant octopus must first digest its food before it can eat again. It is a slow process, and it can take hours for an octopus to eat. This means that it takes time for a giant octopus to gain energy.

When hunting, octopuses extend their tentacles into small crevices. They then use their suckers to feel for food inside.

Life Cycle of the Giant Octopus

Both male and female giant octopuses are able to mate when they are about 32 months old. By this time, they weigh about 33 to 40 pounds (15 to 18 kg). When ready to mate, it is believed that the female releases a chemical that attracts the male. After mating, the female will search for a safe place to lay her eggs.

Over a period of several days, the female octopus will lay between 20,000 and 100,000 eggs in clusters or strings of 200 to 300. The female then hangs these egg strings from the roof of her den. She remains with the eggs and protects her den and the eggs for 7 to 11 months.

The female does not eat once the eggs are hatched. As a result, she usually dies one to two months later. Once the eggs hatch, the **larvae** swim toward the ocean surface. Larvae spend the first months of their lives living near the surface, until they descend to the ocean floor. While living near the surface, the larvae are easy prey. Only a few of them will reach maturity.

Many of a female octopus's eggs will die if not tended by her until hatching.

The Cycle

Octopuses Mate
Giant octopuses mate throughout the year.

Giant Octopuses Reach Maturity
Giant octopuses can live for up to five years.

The Female Lays the Eggs
Females **spawn** only once in their lifetime.

The Eggs Hatch
Larvae are on their own once they hatch. About 1 percent of them will survive to adulthood.

Larvae Grow into Adults
A young octopus increases its weight by 5 percent every day.

History of the Giant Octopus

The oldest **fossil** of an octopus was found in Illinois. It is about 296 million years old. Octopus fossils are rare because octopus bodies are mostly soft. It is difficult for an animal with a soft body to become a fossil. Archaeologists believe that octopuses have been on Earth for more than 300 million years.

Sailors gave the name **Kraken** to the giant octopus, usually telling stories of how the giant creature sank their ships and ate their crew.

Octopuses evolved from an ancestor that had a shell. Over time, octopuses lost most, if not all, of their shell. Some scientists believe this happened so that octopuses could hide from predators. Without a shell, an octopus could burrow into a tighter space to escape from a predator. This also helped the octopus to find prey that was hiding in tight spaces.

There are more than 200 species of octopuses. They are located in all of Earth's oceans. Scientists do not know how many octopuses live in the oceans. Octopuses are not on any endangered species lists.

Stories about the Kraken are believed to date back to 12th century Norway.

Encounters with the Giant Octopus

Divers have been known to encounter the giant octopus while exploring the open seas. Giant octopuses do not generally attack people, but divers have learned to be careful. When a giant octopus reaches out to touch a diver, it is actually using one of its suckers to taste them. If the octopus decides that the diver is food, it can be very difficult for the diver to escape. The giant octopus has also been known to remove diving equipment. Sometimes when this has occurred, the diver has drowned.

Giant octopuses are hunted, mostly in Japan, the Mediterranean, and North America. They are low in fat and high in nutrition. However, it can be challenging for fishers to find them. The octopus's ability to change color can make it difficult to spot.

Sometimes, giant octopuses get caught in commercial fishing nets. When this happens, the giant octopus is often used as bait to catch halibut. Their rubbery octopus flesh can stay on hooks much longer than other kinds of bait.

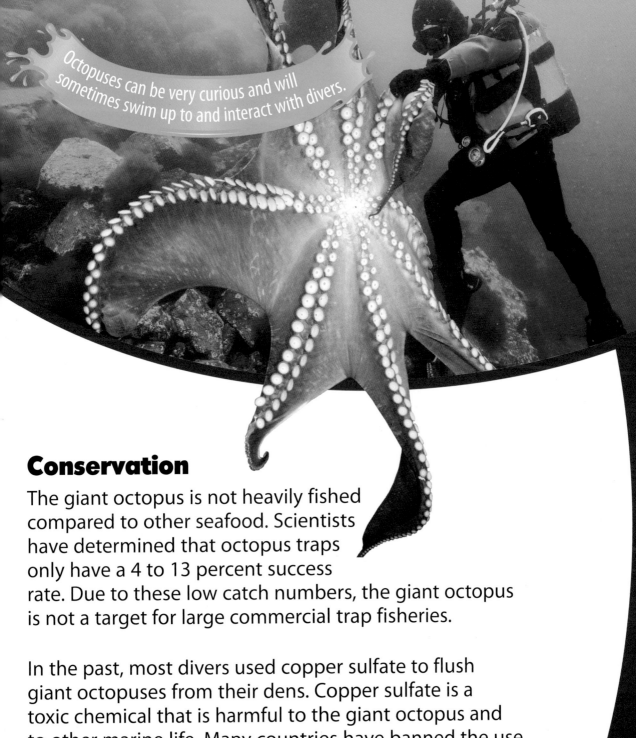

Octopuses can be very curious and will sometimes swim up to and interact with divers.

Conservation

The giant octopus is not heavily fished compared to other seafood. Scientists have determined that octopus traps only have a 4 to 13 percent success rate. Due to these low catch numbers, the giant octopus is not a target for large commercial trap fisheries.

In the past, most divers used copper sulfate to flush giant octopuses from their dens. Copper sulfate is a toxic chemical that is harmful to the giant octopus and to other marine life. Many countries have banned the use of copper sulfate. This has made it difficult for divers to catch the giant octopus.

Myths and Legends

The Legend of Mr. Raven and Miss Octopus

A story from the Aboriginal peoples of the Pacific Northwest warns of the danger of annoying a giant octopus.

One day, a woman was walking along the beach. She had long hair down to her hips that she had braided into eight parts. People called her Miss Octopus. After searching for a while, Miss Octopus found a place that she thought would be good for digging clams. She sat down with her stick and basket and began to dig.

Looking from the village, Mr. Raven saw Miss Octopus out on the beach. He decided to find out what she was doing. When he reached Miss Octopus, he asked, "Are you digging for clams?" Miss Octopus did not answer. She kept digging. Mr. Raven asked her again and again, but Miss Octopus kept quiet and continued with her work.

The tide was coming in, and still Mr. Raven pestered Miss Octopus. Finally, she stood up and faced Mr. Raven. "Yes, I am digging for clams," she said. Her braids then turned into eight long arms. She grabbed Mr. Raven and dragged him underwater.

The people went into the water and found Mr. Raven's body. They took him to a friend who brought him back to life. Mr. Raven never bothered Miss Octopus again.

Test Your Knowledge

There are about 300 octopus species in the world's oceans. The activity below will help you learn more about the different types of these animals. You will need two blank sheets of paper and a pencil or pen.

Materials

Two sheets of Paper   Pencil

1 Using this book and other resources, read about different species of octopus and their characteristics.

2 Now, draw a picture of four different octopus species on the first sheet of paper. Label your drawings with the name of each type of octopus.

3 Across the top of the second sheet of paper, write down the species of the octopuses that you drew. Then, in point form, write down how these species are similar and different from one another.

Quiz

1 How many hearts do giant octopuses have?

2 Why does the giant octopus eject ink?

3 How many types of giant octopus are there?

4 What does the name "octopus" mean?

5 What part of an octopus is made from the same material as human fingernails?

6 Approximately how many suckers does an octopus have on each leg?

7 What is an octopus garden?

8 How many eggs does a female octopus lay?

9 How many years can a giant octopus live?

10 What name did sailors give to the giant octopus?

Answers:
1. Three 2. To escape from predators by masking its scent
3. Three 4. Eight-footed 5. Beak 6. 240
7. A pile of empty shells outside of an octopus's den
8. Between 20,000 and 100,000 9. Up to 5 years
10. Kraken

Key Words

adapted: made changes to be able to live in a particular place or situation

cells: the smallest unit of an organism

class: a taxonomic group of organisms that share a common attribute

fossil: a bone or shell left from animals millions of years ago and saved in rock

gills: an organ that underwater animals use to breath

habitat: the environment in which an organism lives

invertebrates: types of animals that do not have a spinal column

larvae: the earliest stage of development for many types of animals before becoming adults

paralyzes: makes something or someone unable to move

pigment: a material that changes the color of reflected light by absorbing certain wavelengths of the light

predators: animals that prey on others

protein: important molecules inside cells of plants and animals

salivary glands: a body part that produces liquid in the mouth

spawn: to lay a group of eggs in water

species: a group of creatures that have many features in common

toxin: a poison produced by a plant or an animal

Index

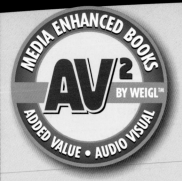

Log on to www.av2books.com

AV² by Weigl brings you media enhanced books that support active learning. Go to www.av2books.com, and enter the special code found on page 2 of this book. You will gain access to enriched and enhanced content that supplements and complements this book. Content includes video, audio, weblinks, quizzes, a slide show, and activities.

AV² Online Navigation

Book Pages
AV² pages directly correspond to pages in the book.

Audio
Listen to sections of the book read aloud.

Video
Watch informative video clips.

Key Words
Study vocabulary, and complete a matching word activity.

Embedded Weblinks
Gain additional information for research.

Quizzes
Test your knowledge.

Slide Show
View images and captions, and prepare a presentation.

Try This!
Complete activities and hands-on experiments.

AV² was built to bridge the gap between print and digital. We encourage you to tell us what you like and what you want to see in the future.

Sign up to be an AV² Ambassador at www.av2books.com/ambassador.